# BEHIND
# THE GREAT WALL

# BEHIND THE GREAT WALL

## A Photographic Essay on China

Black and White Photographs by
### MARY CROSS

Color Photographs by
### THEODORE CROSS

Text by Mary and Theodore Cross

New York

ATHENEUM

1979

# *Acknowledgments*

We would like to express our thanks to all who have in one way or another helped with this book: to Ambassador Mike Mansfield who made arrangements with Peking; to the creative Paul Husted who thought up the voyage and devised the only possible way to get it approved; to Rhoda and Roy Hanson who led our group and so graciously tolerated our truancies; to Grace and Melvin who made us laugh; to the China scholars in New York and Princeton who helped with sociological and artistic detail; to Laura Plaut who provided us with information about sick silkworms in Soochow; to the gracious and ingenious Ted Levenson for his help along the way; to Tony Gigante of Warren, Gorham & Lamont who supported us in all our efforts, to his patience, his good disposition, and fine judgment; to Walter Tower Jr.; to Chet Nightingale who was responsive to our needs for perfection in color and duotone reproduction and kept production running smoothly; to Paul Girouard and Paul Fitzpatrick who skillfully manipulated the subtleties of the four-color press; to Mike Fennelly and Norman Glenn for their excellent judgment and insight into the nuances of two-color printing; to George Curtin, Mike Lynch, Bob Baglione, Kevin Turner, Norma Wilton and all the other members of Nimrod Press who were consistently helpful and cheerful; to Peter Hodges of Warren, Gorham & Lamont who saw the China card before President Jimmy Carter; to Jerry Cross who let us commandeer his office floor; to our editor Marie Orsini; to all who typed, retyped, and checked manuscript, Oyhane Wong, Rochelle Lewis, Elaine Palazzolo, Joann Scanlon. Our thanks especially to Marion Glendining Doyle without whom there would have been no *Behind the Great Wall*.

# Introduction

We would like to tell you a story of modern China. We can only partially capture by photographs its stridency, its self-confidence, its naïve self-deceptions, its *bel canto* horse-opera politics, its remarkable honesty about the property of others, and its thoroughly upbeat young people. These things all contribute to China's formidable charms. Other images are much easier for the photographer to claim: peasants in harness, hauling perhaps a ton of coal; the prancing gait at which they run; the baggy uniforms of the People's Liberation Army; the garish wall posters; the grandiose frescoes in the airports; the old men tenderly playing with their grandchildren; the dignity and authority of old people generally. We have put a camera on many of these things.

Other images keep coming back, some which were photographed and some which escaped: the tens of thousands of bicycle riders who, as in a trance, move like shadows through Peking's T'ien An Men Square; the peasants, so proud of their wristwatches, hunkered down and deep in conversation; the endless cigarette smoking, hawking, and spitting; the interminable mugs of green tea. Indelibly etched are the glimpses through the willow trees of water buffaloes and peasants plowing in the rice paddies. No visitor can forget the sunflowers, the banyan trees, the sky, and the oppressive tropical heat of the South China coast.

China's images, too, are the sights one expects to see but does not. Suddenly, one realizes there are no birds, no flies, no drunks, no beggars, no panhandlers, and almost no dogs or cats. Gone, too, are the singing pet crickets old men used to carry around in cages. Remembering one's own country, one notices, too, that there are no sex shops, prostitutes, hustlers, or drug pushers. With some sadness, one misses, in this prudish society, not having the challenge of surreptitiously taken photographs of kisses exchanged between young lovers. One sees women with babies, yes, but where are the *mothers* holding small children by the hand? But these are things that are *not* there, and there is no way to photograph a void.

Again, one returns to things of the past which may not be recorded on film. Gone are the putrid cities with the stench of the dead. Gone from the children's heads are the flies and the scalp sores of poor nutrition. No more do people by the millions die in famines after a single year of grain failure. Today, an old woman with a horrible pain goes to a hospital instead of dying in a ditch. The state no longer permits the drowning of unwanted babies. No more "medals of honor" posthumously awarded to wives who committed suicide in shame for not producing a male child. No young women today are sold into sexual bondage or domestic slavery. Gone is the cruel and stupid pomp of the mandarinate with their 4-inch long fingernails, hat spikes, jewels, and peacock feathers. Almost no one bothered to photograph the horrible insensitivities and misery of the past. Now, they are gone.

Even as we concentrate on images rather than politics, the euphoric vision of huge progress in this country cannot obscure the terrible losses of liberty. The tourist may leave China when he has had enough; the Chinese citizen cannot. Chinese workers are assigned to jobs which they may not quit. Until the state says otherwise, they live and work where they are born. The ration book, good only for the local allotment of rice, imprisons the citizen and prevents him, without permission, from visiting relatives in another place. In South Africa, we photographed wives and their husbands on whom family separation was enforced in the interests of racial apartheid. In China, the same thing happens in the interests of the greater efficiency of an inefficient state. But no loneliness shows on the recorded picture of the face of a Chinese man who is permitted to see his wife only once every two months.

China declares that she will now borrow American technology, but not her liberties. Personal freedoms are our values, not theirs. Yet we must stand in awe at the successes, stunning by their standards or our own, of the most world-shaking social experiment in the recent history of mankind.

When in the history of humanity has there been a precedent for the increase, in only thirty years' time, of life expectancies from thirty to sixty years?

There is a lighter side to visiting China. Of endless amusement and fascination for the visitor is the colorful and bombastic way which China brings to the problem of maintaining a totalitarian state. Universal obedience to the commands of the Party requires an absolute consensus. People must think alike, act alike, live alike, love alike, and (at any particular time) despise and venerate the same people. But consensus is not always achieved. There is, in fact, constant verbal and poster warfare to establish orthodoxy. Invectives, rather than reason, are weapons in this war. The result is that no day passes in which the traveler to China is not treated to a delicious collection of epithets. The most creative of these are found in the big character posters. The visitors' vocabulary will be expanded to include such useful and satisfying phrases as, "Cut off their dogheads," or better yet, "Kick the dogs while they are in the water," "Blast these insects," "Destroy these pests, scabs, henchmen, and hegemonists," "They have honey on their lips and murder in their hearts."

These references, of course, are not to western capitalists but to fellow Marxists, Russian or Chinese, who have not recognized that which, for the moment, is the correct and pure and final form of state socialism. The end of the Gang of Four has not put an end to China's remarkable penchant for rhetoric.

As China now opens up after thirty years of isolation from the outside world, there is a tendency to interpret events, as well as the images one sees and records, in apocalyptic terms. But China is a country which may not be judged in the same frame of reference as other great nations. Unlike the United States, she measures her history in thousands, rather than hundreds, of years. The duration to date of the Great Revolution occupies only 1/100 of her recorded history. Apparently, she numbers her towns and villages in the hundreds of thousands instead of tens of thousands. The 850 million agrarian peasant Chinese who struggle from dawn to dusk to survive today do so with essentially the same technology of the ox and wooden plow as were used by their ancestors, who also lived on the brink of famine. For 3,000 years, China has been an introverted nation, self-sufficient and contemptuous of the West. Why, after three millenniums of no change, may we assume that China will become a superpower by the year 2000? For the past century or more, China has had many periods when she acquired a sudden "crush" on things western, only to turn inward once again.

It is the huge and unfamiliar scale of this nation which throws us off guard as to what, in realistic terms, is likely to occur. China apparently plans to spend by 1985 upward to $800 *billion* in the "Four Modernizations." This is an astronomical sum which even central bankers cannot comprehend. But it is merely $800 per Chinese citizen and, as such, less than one-ninth of the per-capita income of a citizen of the United States in a single year. Perhaps, too, China may succeed in what superficially appears to be a modest goal of adding one pound of grain per week to each citizen's ration. This incremental amount of grain would be equal to the entire annual consumption of the United States.

The huge scale of the Chinese nation is matched by the scale of her kind attention to Westerners. The traveler to the Soviet Union is likely to meet up with many sullen and unfriendly people. But China is different. The Westerner is truly a *privileged* person. Even before diplomatic recognition, we felt enveloped by the warmth and kindness of the Chinese people.

One afternoon in Shanghai, we were lost. A little boy, who spoke no English, saw our confusion. He took us by the hand, beckoning us to follow him. He conducted us through two bus transfers, led us to the doorstep of our hotel, and waved good-bye.

One morning at six, as we wandered along the moat outside Peking's Forbidden City, a twenty-year-old Chinese student approached us and, obviously practicing his English, asked our nationality. We answered: "American," "Then you are our friends," he responded. This touching gesture occurred four months before President Carter's announcement of the normalization of relations between the United States and China. This is not politically motivated hospitality.

Go to China! Everywhere you will be offered the hand of friendship. This is a remarkable change in attitude in a nation which is reputed capable of bearing the loss of anything but the loss of face. We wonder how she can forgive us the miserable John Foster Dulles, who, at the Geneva Conference in 1954, turned away from the hand of friendship offered by Chou En-lai.

The first job of the photographer who would bring back images of China is to discover what China is not. The real China is not the Stalinesque grandeur of the Peking Hotel. It is not the children at the "show schools" clapping on command to welcome foreign visitors. It is not the apple-cheeked girl posed among the tea bushes to satisfy western preconceptions of the ideal Chinese woman. It is not pigs bathed and curried twenty minutes before an American tour visits the show commune. All these things are the Potemkin villages which the government uses to deceive and propagandize.

China's pulse may and must be taken in unsupervised visits to the streets, villages, and countryside. China is a nation of card players and old men squatting on tiny bamboo stools playing Chinese chess under street lights. China is young people helping old women with bound feet to cross a bustling street. It is soldiers exchanging jokes as they watch the tourists at the Great Wall. It is a grandfather patiently feeding noodles to his grandson. It is tens of millions of peasants endlessly squatting in the rice paddies.

Our goal here is to present a varied and rich cross-section of Chinese life. We sought photographs of all ages, from gnarled old women to fat babies in bamboo carriages. We set out to present a balance of urban and rural scenes. Our strategy was to head for back streets. Without guides, we rode all over Shanghai on public trolleys and buses. We placed ourselves in sections of the world's largest city where Westerners have rarely been. We got up 5:30 each morning and hiked the streets, finding Chinese doing exercises, wrestling, and solemnly practicing musical instruments. We made a special effort to photograph old people. They are the only vestiges of old China. They, too, will soon be gone.

The reader will find only one photograph recording the "approved" factory tours. Risking criticism by our American friends for being "uncooperative" and having "bad" attitudes, we escaped from our organized group whenever we could. We hired taxis in every city. We visited three communes instead of the scheduled five, three factories instead of five, and only two Buddhist temples instead of six.

We searched for the private street capitalist, the popsicle vendor, the vegetable seller, the purveyor of Chinese dumplings. We looked for weaknesses to balance the proudly displayed strengths; women yoked together, a man recovering from tuberculosis, a woman struggling to pull heavy wooden garbage vats, an elderly gentleman in Manchu dress, his politics as unreconstructed as his beard. We photographed overcrowded lilongs (alleys) where forty or more families may live, sharing outdoor faucets, basins, and privies.

In a world which is increasingly inhospitable to western ways of life, there are temptations to be judgmental about what one sees in China. In this book, we make no judgment other than an expression of endless fascination for these people who are striving, "intensely," as the Chinese say, to give content to the most ambitious dream which has possessed any civilization in modern times.

MARY AND THEODORE CROSS

March 1, 1979

*To Amanda, Ann, Garny,*
*Lisa, Polly, Stuart*

*and to Dorothy and Bill*

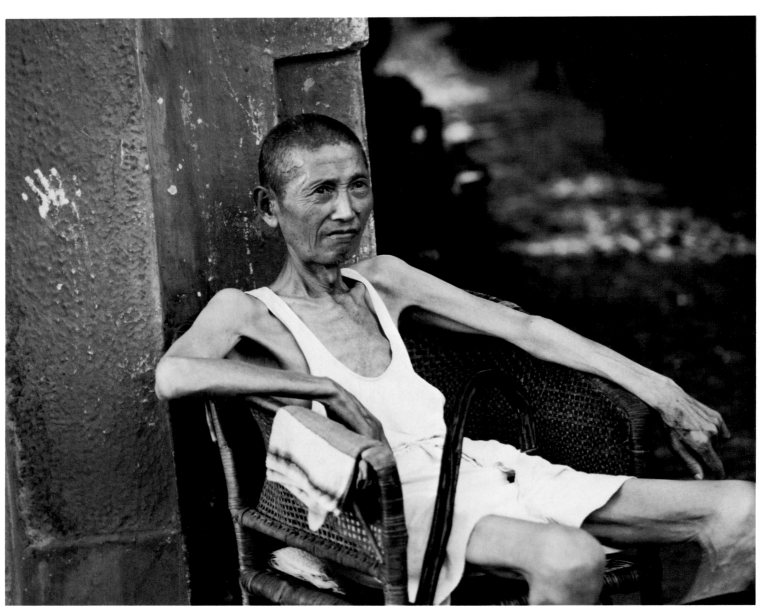

7

11

13

15

## 1 Gate of Heavenly Peace

It was in October 1949 that Chairman Mao Tse-tung solemnly proclaimed the founding of the People's Republic of China from the magnificent T'ien An Men Gate. Every day, Chinese citizens by the thousands pass through this great portal once again to see the greater poster of Mao (complete with mole on his chin), look up to the balcony where he spoke, and recommit themselves to the spirit of the great proletarian revolution.

## 2 A Lilong in Shanghai

The distended bellies of starving children are gone. No longer does Shanghai smell of rotting human flesh. But, by western standards, poverty is still the essential Chinese condition.

A lilong (alley) shown here provides a home for over forty families.

Red Guards may go on the rampage and cultural revolutions convulse the country, but, in this Shanghai working-class community, the populace worries about ration books, spying by neighborhood guards and committees, and saving enough yuan to buy a sewing machine or a bicycle.

These families have no indoor plumbing; they use a communal toilet adjacent to their building. They cool their food in a well and get their water from a community cold-water spigot. Cooking is done in shared kitchens on small braziers. The fuel is a combination of compacted mud and coal dust.

One bare lightbulb of low wattage hangs nakedly from the ceiling, providing dim illumination. In summer, no air stirs in the poorly ventilated apartments, one reason the populace takes to the streets for card playing, gossip, dice, or reading.

The laundry hanging above the alley shows the recent trend toward new styles and patterns. Plaids, flower prints, and brightened colors are now officially sanctioned and provide a relief from the drabness of white shirts and dark pants.

## 3 The Tattered Coat

This peasant lives and works in an agricultural commune outside of Shanghai. Possessing new clothes may suggest undesirable bourgeois traits; making do with old and tattered clothing is a distinct virtue. Besides, there is no other choice. The patches on his thirty-year-old jacket are a collage of his life as a farm laborer.

In strong contrast to the rest of the country, Shanghai, China's most cosmopolitan city, has managed to maintain a modicum of fashion and style. Even in the ubiquitous white shirt or tunic blouse, the Shanghai tailor manages to inject a subtle bit of flair.

## 4 Woman With Scale

Careful to be precise and "scrupulously honest," this Cantonese woman weighs vegetables on an ancient hand scale.

Jewelry is rarely seen in the People's Republic, but some older women wear tiny gold rings in their pierced ears. Occasionally, one sees a wedding band.

## 5 Chinese Trawlers

Every Red Chinese fishing boat also serves as an official Red Chinese coast guard vessel. Manned by mean characters with grappling hooks, some do spying as well as smuggling on the side.

## 6 Flutist

Chinese music normally assaults western ears with shrill, sing-song dissonance. The children display their musical talents on bizarre instruments such as the pipa, a kind of lute, and the erhu, a two-string violin.

At 6:00 A.M., beneath the willows by the moat of the Imperial Palace in Peking, a young factory worker studiously disciplines himself with the more tranquil notes of the flute. The city is quiet and t'ai chi ch'üan exercises are still in progress.

## 7 Tuberculosis

This middle-aged man shows the ravages of tuberculosis.

During the early 1950s, infectious, parasitic, and epidemic diseases killed an estimated four million Chinese each year. These afflictions have largely been eliminated, along with cholera, smallpox, and plague.

Particularly in the winter and spring, northern China continues to be a hospitable environment for respiratory problems: There is intense crowding, some malnutrition, and always cold air and choking yellow dust blowing in from the Gobi Desert.

Bacteria and viruses are distributed among the people by the widespread Chinese custom of unrestrained expectoration. It is highly acceptable to hawk, spit, and blow one's nose without benefit of handkerchief. If asked about these habits, which most westerners find repugnant, the Chinese respond: "Why blow your infection into a rag and then preserve it in your pocket?"

## 8 Neighborhood Canteen

A Cantonese woman serves tea in a canteen operated by a neighborhood committee. The fast-food canteen serves workers during their break and alleviates the heavy domestic burden of working Chinese women. Canteen food is inexpensive; a family can afford to eat there several times a week.

There are no flies in the kitchen. Pests, including mosquitoes, were eliminated long ago by issuing flyswatters to the entire population.

Probably, the Chinese eat out more than any other people. The *Shanghai Daily* reports that Shanghai alone has 12,000 restaurants and that more than half the population of Canton eats breakfast outside the home. At the canteens, the usual eating position is standing up, leaning against a counter, or sitting on one's haunches.

There are three requirements for good cooking: "good color, good fragrance, and good flavor." The rules are observed in the canteens as well as in the homes.

## 9 Touring the Great Wall

In Chinese metaphor, the People's Liberation Army is China's "Great Wall." The frenzy about Russian "hegemony" is not unwarranted. A million Soviet troops are stationed along the northern China border.

Instead of serving as a traditional refuge of the unemployed, membership in the Army is coveted. Workers and peasants are favored candidates; people of bourgeois or landlord ancestry are excluded. The PLA is closely tied with the Communist Party and makes arrests for political crimes. Until late 1978, the army controlled admission to higher education. Now rigorous and competitive examinations have been reinstated for college admission.

The Great Wall, 2,400 miles long, the largest piece of construction ever executed by man, was built by slave labor. The Wall has been restored at three famous points, including Pataling Pass, north of Peking. Here is an excellent example of Ming military architecture. At the upper left, there is a two-story tower with an observation platform above and guard room below. The pathway up the wall is occasionally broken by steep steps. People's Liberation Army soldiers have a tradition of running up the wall, a show of manliness as they race past exhausted and breathless civilians.

The Wall was chiefly defensive, but it doubled as a communication route. Great communities of soldiers and their families could move quickly through mountainous areas. In most areas, the top of the Wall was wide enough to accommodate five horses abreast.

## 10 Peasant Soldiers

These People's Liberation Army soldiers came from peasant stock. On the subject of the Soviet Union, they are hysterical: "The Russians have honey on their lips and murder in their hearts."

This may not be paranoia in a civilization which has successfully kept its culture alive since the time when Europe was inhabited by barbarians.

## 11 The New Curriculum

For fifty million or more Chinese children, the Cultural Revolution (1966-1970) was a tragedy. All schools were closed for four years. Teachers were castigated as elitist and shipped off to communes to learn proper proletarian attitudes from the peasants. Many educators, writers, and intellectuals committed suicide. During this period, all scientific, cultural, and literary pursuits ceased. The children of the late sixties, who are now late teen-agers and young adults, are more proficient at mouthing political jargon than at applying themselves to engineering or production.

Recent edicts from Peking restore the prestige, titles, and authority of the teaching profession. This Shanghai child will go to school six days a week, six hours a day. Recent political changes will reintroduce science, foreign language, and world history into the curriculum but her Chinese language courses will continue to be based on Mao Tse-tung's simplistic prose. There will be little pursuit of knowledge for the sake of "pure knowing."

## 12 The Great Helmsman Watches Badminton

When Shanghai was the captive city of European imperialism, this elegant mansion was the home of a western merchant. The marble halls converted into a children's palace now echo with the sound of children's voices singing, dancing, and acting in political dramas. The mansion provides a training ground in music, ballet, drama, and graphic arts. The school turns out "technically" competent musicians and artists. Mozart's "Eine Kline Nacht Musik" is performed here with uninspired precision. One questions how much originality and creativity is possible in a school where the person in charge states, and apparently believes, that "all the children play the piano equally well."

For these children, there are no fairy stories about frogs turning into princes. Zeal and militance are the grist of their childhood songs. In the classrooms, they become automatons. Their teachers boast: "These children will never send a single soldier to invade and occupy another country. . . . They will never demand a single military base from any country. They will never extort a single penny from another nation or hold it up to ransom. . . . No matter how the superpowers huff and puff, these children will be the gravediggers of the hegemonists."

In the halls, a wild badminton game takes place; the children are seemingly quite free to jump around and be noisy and silly.

There are children's palaces all over China with the same programs of arts and special education. The painted poster in the background portrays the probably apocryphal event when the dying Chairman Mao turned over control of the state to Hua. He is alleged to have said: "With you in charge, I am at ease."

## 13 The Tricycle Cab

As a traditional symbol of exploitation and servitude, the rickshaw has been banned in the People's Republic. But there is no stigma attached to pedaling one's own family or friends in a three-wheeled tricycle cab, except in Peking, where they have been banned.

As long as China remains backward, human motor power will supply the bulk of the nation's energy.

## 14 Outside the East Happiness Coop

Canton is a town of lively neighborhoods. Its covered arcades are jammed with small manufacturing enterprises of basket weaving, rope making, canteens, wine shops, blacksmiths, and vegetable markets. School is out from July to September, and teen-agers swarm the streets.

The women who balance heavy loads on bamboo poles usually wear shoulder pads; they walk with light prancing steps that set the suspended baskets springing in measured cadence.

Since dogs and cats compete with humans for food, there are few such pets in Chinese cities. Farmers raise dogs for slaughter, eat the meat, and send off the pelts to be made into quilts. Dogs are occasionally used as herd animals and can be seen out the train windows on the ride between Canton and the New Territories. Cats are found almost exclusively in zoos. The authors saw three cats during their entire trip. Since the first priority in China is food, there are no protected bird species and almost no birds.

## 15 Hunchback

A hunchback worker ambles through Canton streets on the way to his job. Citizens with physical handicaps are exempted from heavy labor, but all able-bodied citizens perform some daily work. This gentleman is prepared for the scorching Cantonese sun of August or the equal possibility of a sudden downpour.

## 16 Child on Her Grandfather's Bamboo Chaise

According to ancient Chinese custom dating back 2,500 years, a child is one year old at birth. All birthdays are celebrated on January first, so a child born in December officially becomes two years old on New Year's Day. These festivities may be held privately, but they are frowned upon by the neighborhood committees. Individual birthdays take time away from "carrying out the general tasks of the revolution." Cakes and gifts are considered an extravagance.

Too bad about her birthday. But huge comfort in the fact that she won't be sold to a rich peasant to be raised as a servant.

## 17 Manchu Traditionalist

The Cultural Revolution attacked the "four olds"—"old culture, old customs, old habits, and old thoughts"—but never old people.

This gentleman, who was elderly before liberation, could pass for Jui-lin, Manchu Governor-General of Kwang-tung (c. 1868). Supported by the government and living in a retirement home, he wears a traditional beard and an old-fashioned Chinese blouse. Regarded as quaint but harmless, a thought-reform session would not begin to touch his traditional consciousness of "the proper order of things."

## 18 Shanghai Transfer Company

Chinese talents in the fine arts of balancing show in their transportation, as well as their acrobatics and tumbling. They stack everything and everyone on the back of a tricycle. Here, the freight dispatcher has stowed a towering load of brand new office chairs with utmost confidence that the furniture will arrive unscathed.

Truckers in the West would require a half-ton truck to achieve the same result. Notice that, unlike in some countries, furniture moving in China is not a profession closed to women.

## 19 Ultimate Supreme Boxing

Physical fitness is part of the politics of China. Twice a day in early morning and before lunch, almost all citizens participate in some form of calisthenics or other physical exercise. Here, in front of a Peking bookstore, we see the "ultimate supreme boxing" (t'ai chi ch'üan). This snakelike series of 128 basic bodily movements originated as a combat discipline for fitness. Every muscle of the body is exercised in the fifteen minutes required for its performance. The participants seem to enjoy the routinized sequence of gestures. T'ai chi ch'üan is as much a part of Chinese life as sleeping and eating. Jogging is on the increase. Chinese often jog in plastic sandals, a practice destined to produce bone bruises.

## 20 The Finest Teeth

Unusually healthy teeth are the result of a low-sugar diet and government-encouraged toothpicking and brushing. This Cantonese worker displays a set of the finest.

Peking has signed a recent trade agreement with the Coca-Cola Company, giving it an exclusive franchise for cola sales in China. Coca-Cola executives are licking their chops as they contemplate the prospect of half a billion Cokes sold in a single day.

Good-bye Chinese balance of payments! Good-bye Chinese teeth!

Another superior trait is good eyesight. Children in China do a series of daily eye exercises; they are given eyedrops every morning in school. Almost no Chinese youngsters wear eyeglasses, a circumstance which has caused American ophthalmologists to speculate as to whether a lot of Chinese children walk around with impaired vision.

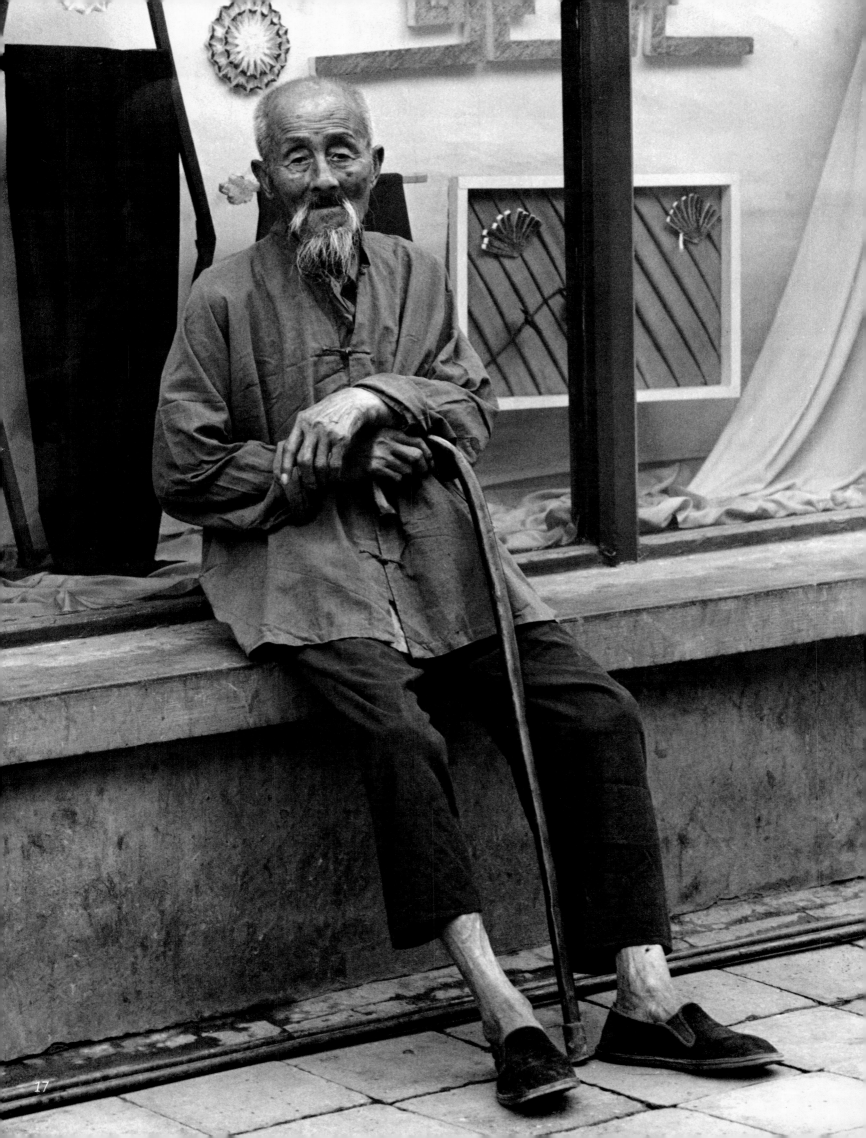

19

22

26

## 21 Chairman Mao Brings the Spring

Like other good things, "Chairman Mao brings the spring." The message of this political wall poster dominates a large open square in Canton near the Tung Fang "The East is Red" Hotel. It is unlikely that any visitor to China will escape the Tung Fang (formerly the Sino-Soviet Friendship Hotel). The hotel buildings are huge charmless concrete barracks. Each room has one thermos bottle, one electric fan, and grimy uncarpeted concrete floors. Each bathroom is provided with a telephone near the toilet so foreign merchants can make business deals.

Below the giant poster is a hexagonal structure with vertical stripes. This is a traffic control police booth. Loudspeakers on the booth enable the traffic officer to criticize cyclists and pedestrians who violate the codes. There are speed limits for bicycles and other vehicles, but everyone travels at breakneck speed.

The government poster billboards are ubiquitous. They publish saccharin and empty rhetoric such as: "Sailing the seas depends on the helmsman," or "Struggle to carry out the general tasks of the revolution." The posters contain no real information as to who are the current heroes or "bad eggs" in the Politburo. Most recent posters deal with the "Four Modernizations."

Real clues to current government attitudes are discovered in the polemics of big character posters painted and posted by Chinese citizens. The Chinese Government is sometimes permissive about free expression on the "democracy wall" site at the intersection of Chan An Avenue and Hsi Tan Street in Peking. This area is frequently compared to Hyde Park Corner in London. News of who is to be disgraced, discarded, or rehabilitated is first posted here. When big character posters calling for the purge of Wang and Wu, for example, are allowed to remain, it is likely that Wang and Wu soon will be leaving their jobs in the Politburo. The famous November 19, 1978 citizen poster accusing Mao Tse-tung of having been a supporter of the "Gang of Four" signaled the start of a government campaign to demythologize Mao.

Most posters soon end up in the rubbish carts of the poster removal squads which operate in every city. The posters which get pulled down first may be the ones which urge an intolerable suggestion such as a call for elections by secret ballot or criticize a party leader whose star is in the ascendancy. Under no circumstances may the fundamental tenets of Marxism be criticized. To find out what is going on, one waits to see how long a particular writing will be allowed to stay on the wall.

For many weeks in early 1979, posters calling on American President Jimmy Carter to help Chinese citizens win their basic human rights were allowed to remain on the Hsi Tan Wall. Unquestionably, citizen posters serve as a safety valve against more serious protest. It is universally gratifying to see one's name in print for the first time.

Vice Premier Teng Hsiao-ping has declared that big character posters are allowed by the country's constitution. Here is a man of principle, for it was frenetic poster campaigns which twice purged him as a "capitalist roader," who was pushing modernization at the expense of revolutionary purity.

## 22 Sampan on Canton's Pearl River

An old-fashioned sampan powered by a small sail moves down the Pearl River.

The sign on the building reads: "Unite, struggle for greater victory."

The most despised members of a caste system, 60,000 people used to live and die on wretched boats and barges in Canton. Known as "the boat people," they were prisoners on the river. Shunned by Cantonese citizenry, they were never allowed ashore.

John Thompson, the pioneer photographer of Imperial China, wrote in 1873 that the boat people were better off on their sampans because otherwise they would be crowded in makeshift hovels breathing the polluted air of a city where all sanitary regulations were ignored.

The Peking Government today makes a probably exaggerated claim that all the "boat people have been rehabilitated."

## 23 Crones in Black

With sensible attention to maximizing agricultural labor, these Cantonese peasant women were permitted to escape the excruciating tortures of bound feet. They were also spared the less painful but more permanent custom of infanticide by drowning.

Lives of toil produce the vascular swellings known in China as "elephant legs."

The woman on the right has a patch on her temple which covers a curative herbal balm. She believes the natural elixir will seep through the skin over her temple and banish her headache.


## 24  *The Haichu Bridge*

Canton's Haichu Bridge spans the Pearl River. It was rebuilt after the original was destroyed by Chiang Kai-shek's armies in 1949. The Pearl, South China's largest river, carries huge volumes of murky yellow water and waste to the sea. So rapid is the current that the schoolboys who dive in the river resurface 30 yards downstream. Their bobbing black heads look like tiny swimming ants. During the ebb tide, small sampans and barges jam the river with traffic. A boatman maneuvers his small craft downstream; he has no choice but to move with the current.


## 25  *New Freedoms*

"The purpose of 'liquidate illiteracy' is only that every peasant should be able to read by himself, without help, our decrees, orders and proclamations. The aim is completely practical."
                                                              —Vladimir Ilyitch Lenin

In Canton, a young woman reads the *Guangchow Daily*, Canton's only newspaper.

She is strong, rosy-cheeked, with straight black hair, and, if she is married, definitely using her maiden name. If Napoleon's predictions that China will someday awake come true, it is young women like this who "will make the world tremble."

Access to the Chinese local press has been forbidden to foreigners, who are allowed to read the national press *(People's Daily, Kuangming Daily,* and the *Red Flag)*. All news of sports events, art exhibits, and cultural happenings are only published in the local *Peking Daily.* The result is that foreign diplomats who lived in Peking have been unable to find out what is happening.

Posted daily in glass cases for every citizen to read, the newspapers are full of traditional party jargon, Maoist doctrine, and rewarmed rhetoric.

During the November 1978 public demonstrations and the frenzy of hanging large character wall posters in Peking, angry citizens told western reporters that they did not believe what they read in the newspapers. There were impassioned speeches calling for freedom of the press. Proof that civil rights does not yet extend to free speech was the fact that posters calling for this great liberty were torn down from Hsi Tan Wall, put up again and then torn down once again.

A more liberal attitude exists toward foreign writings and information about America. Peking University's English reading room has uncensored U.S. newspapers and magazines on reserve. In the old days, anyone caught listening to the Voice of America could be sent to a reform camp. English language programs are no longer being jammed. The Chinese are now fearlessly asking for textbooks to help them with the Voice's lessons in English language.

Chinese journalists from Hsinhua, the Chinese press agency, have recently written truthful and candid articles after a visit to the United States. They reported America to be a land of urban decay, spacious parks, well-run subways, and freak religious cults.


## 26  *The Obelisk*

In summer, water trucks cool down the Peking streets several times a day. The heat is fierce in the glare of the midday sun on T'ien An Men Square. Behind this three-wheeled cart stands an obelisk, over 100 feet in height, erected by Chairman Mao as a monument to the Heroes of the People. It was constructed after Mao had demolished much of Peking's traditional architecture, including the city walls and a series of magnificent gates. "Destroy the old to establish the new" was the prescription to make way for broad sterile boulevards and the vast wastelands of open public squares. Peking's elegant past has been decimated.

Today, there are only vast open spaces filled with millions of gliding black bicycles. One sees a few 1930s-style grey touring cars used exclusively for very important Chinese governmental officials and touring diplomats from abroad.

## 27  Chinese at Play on Kunming Lake

Chinese life is not all toil. Everyday is "Sunday" for one-seventh of the work force. At Kunming Lake, a part of the fairyland Summer Palace outside of Peking, Chinese citizens rent rowboats and take each other's pictures with rented cameras.

## 28  Marx and Engels

One billion Oriental people still organize their lives according to the theories of two nineteenth century German intellectuals, Karl Marx and Friedrich Engels.

## 29  The Stone Boat

Diverting funds intended to upgrade China's deteriorating navy, the Dowager Empress Tz-u-hsi in 1888 remodeled the 700-acre Summer Palace north of Peking along with its famous Stone Boat. The Chinese tourists love her insane creation.

The Dowager Empress (1835-1908) was the Chinese counterpart of Queen Victoria. Born with the name "Little Orchid" (Lan Kuei) to a minor Manchurian official, at age 17 she achieved the coveted position of concubine to Emperor Hsien Feng. In this exalted position, she lived with the Emperor in the royal household of 6,000 women and eunuchs. Sometime in 1855, according to the erotic handbooks of the time, the Emperor turned "face up" the jade tablet bearing her name which lay on a table outside her bedroom. This symbolized the Emperor's decision to jettison the then current empress who was barren, in favor of the superior sexual prowesses of Little Orchid. Given the signal, the chief eunuch then wrapped the 20-year-old concubine in a red rug and carried her to the foot of the Emperor's bed. She crawled to the head of the bed to meet the Emperor's lustful embrace.

Forty-five years later, this doughty (and dotty) little woman declared war on nine nations, the United States of America, France, Great Britain, Germany, Italy, Austria, Belgium, Holland, and Japan.

She lost!

## 30  Canton's Renaissance Architecture

Early in the sixteenth century, the Portuguese introduced European architecture into the port of Canton. Since then, China's architectural history has been one of subjection to western influence. Ionic columns borrowed from Greece and Oriental fretwork meld in a harmonious mélange of East and West.

Housing has been the great failure of the Revolutionary government. These quasi-Italian renaissance buildings have not been repaired in decades. Makeshift electric wiring runs along the outside of the buildings. These outwardly elegant apartment buildings may house three families in one three-room flat. Above the shopping arcades, each family has small potted herb gardens on their balconies. In the summer when school is out, Cantonese children swarm the streets and arcades dodging in and out among the bicycles, tricycle carts, busses, and trucks and, from now on, American tourists.

## 31  Hemp Worker

Here is a typical Cantonese face with protruding but straight teeth and thickish lips. She is a weaver. Working with hemp, the primary crop in South China, she wears a traditional costume of baggy shirt and loose-fitting pants. Although uneducated and untrained, she regularly attends neighborhood committee meetings. You can be sure her attitudes are correct.

In a market economy such as the United States, the worker is free to find the employment that suits him or her best. In China, the worker accepts the employment which best suits the state. This is the great difference in freedoms. Nowhere in China has the loss of this great liberty been mourned. For, unlike us, they never had it in the first place.

## 32  The Accordion Player

It is early morning in Peking, but the summer heat is already scorching along the willow-lined pathway by the moat near the Imperial Palace. The city's 2 million bicycles and tens of thousands of heavy trucks carrying workers to the communes have not yet upset the serenity of the moment. Early morning strollers are captivated by a school child playing his accordion on loan from a children's palace school.

In the evening, Peking citizens abandon their work clothes and jump in the moat for a cooling midnight swim.

## 33 *Watching the Boats on Kunming Lake*

Kunming Lake and the Summer Palace, seven kilometers north of Peking, provide endless delights for Chinese from all walks of life. Here, leaning on the ornate balustrade, are a soldier of the People's Liberation Army, a two-year-old child with his father, and three school girls in their teens. The objects of intense study and fascination are the rowboats in the lake below.

## 34 *Young Married Couple*

In the days of mourning after the death of Mao, young couples were seen holding hands, a rare event in puritanical China. Recently, it has been reported that public handholding is on the increase. But even married people generally do not allow themselves outward displays of affection.

It is probable that this young Peking couple chose each other without much parental influence. He was over 27; she was over 25. They met, decided they liked each other, went to the revolutionary committee of their commune, and were questioned as to their political beliefs. Once pronounced ideologically suited, they spent more time together, taking walks and joining together in brigade activities.

At last, they were married. Rings were not exchanged. If the bride received the universally coveted sewing machine for a wedding gift, she would consider it the fulfillment of her most fanciful desires. The ceremony was simple. The bride and groom bowed to their elders and then sat down to a simple country luncheon. A bowl of glutinous noodles was the only remnant of old customs symbolizing a hope that the couple would stick closely together. The official record of the marriage was listed in the commune record.

In old China, a bride was frequently sold into matrimonial bondage. Traditionally, her new mother-in-law was cruel and demanding. She frequently took sadistic pleasure in beating her new daughter-in-law. If a wife failed to produce a male offspring, an additional wife was purchased. Until 1950, unwanted female infants were sometimes drowned like puppies in a sack.

Under the 1950 marriage law, the government abolished the feudal marriage system. Child betrothals, forced marriage, bigamy, and concubinage are outlawed. Now, widows may remarry, and wives may ask for divorce.

## 35 *Husband and Wife From the Old Regime*

This Shanghai couple was married before Liberation. They remember the days when Shanghai was a fiefdom of western powers. It was a city of international trade, intrigue, casinos, opium dens and brothels. In the sections of Shanghai reserved for foreigners, signs read: "No dogs or Chinese allowed."

Change is everywhere. People rub their eyes in constant amazement. Shanghai women have been seen wearing bright pink and magenta lipstick. Shanghai beauty parlors charge $2.50 for a shampoo and set. Tangerine and fuschia brassieres can be found in department stores. Movie theaters are showing foreign films. These gentle old people would prefer to be left alone to grow old in a traditional and non-political manner.

## 36 *Chinese Tourists Ride the Train*

Egalitarianism breaks down in the Chinese trains. There are three choices: "sitting hard" (ying tso), "sleeping hard" (ying wo), and "sleeping soft" (juan wo). Fares are much higher in the "soft" cars.

First-class accommodations are reserved for western visitors, foreign guests, and high cadre officials. Even by western standards, the "soft" cars are very comfortable. Between two banks of seats are tea tables, each graced with a live bonsai tree. Tea is served in delicate, covered tea mugs decorated with willow or bamboo designs. Each seat is covered with an immaculate white slip cover with an elegantly pleated skirt. On the window are lace curtins. The car doors are kept locked to prevent the admission of the hoi polloi.

36

40

44

This police officer maintains order on a train which runs from Peking to the Great Wall. The armband signifies that he is on duty, but his trip will be uneventful.

Westerners, who glorify China as a nation free from crime, are not entirely naïve. Shanghai visitors do walk the unlit streets of the largest city in the world at night with no fear of mugging. Valuables are completely safe in unlocked hotel rooms in Peking, Shanghai, and Kweilin. The authors have seen a Chinese citizen pick up a lost bank note on the street and turn it over to a traffic officer on the corner who called, through his loudspeaker, for the owner to reclaim the bill.

Part of the reason for the honesty is the Chinese system of mutual spying. Turning people in improves one's status with the neighborhood committee, as well as one's opportunity to get a job as an official. Also, private possessions of value are so rare that if a citizen showed up with a new (stolen) watch or bicycle, everyone in his neighborhood or commune would know how he got it.

People save money for years to buy such treasured possessions as a sewing machine or a transistor radio. These acquisitions are a cause of great celebration. No wonder the thief gets turned in by his peers.

Known criminal elements in China are disaffected youths who, in the past, were sent to the country to work. Lacking a rice coupon book, these so-called vagabonds secretly return to the cities and support themselves by stealing.

Other criminal groups are "Shanghai types," black marketeers, who trade in ration books and barter with foreigners in contraband, jade jewelry, and works of art. For the less heinous economic crimes, the punishment is reeducation, forced public confessions, humiliation before one's peers, an agreement to work harder, and a promise to acquire a better knowledge of socialist principles.

Political prisoners, according to Amnesty International, are routinely starved, put in chains, and held in solitary confinement. Trials are a formality and are, "in fact, meetings to announce the sentence."

China has recently announced the intention of setting up a new legal system that will guarantee public trials and modify criminal and civil codes. Peking promises this will unify criminal law and will end political persecution, secret trials, and the fear of harassment without recourse to law.

## 38  *Mr. Hsiu and the Buddha*

Mr. Hsiu Li-kong, an expert on the nuances of current party dogma, sits on the lap of a fourteenth century Buddhist bas relief in Hangchow. A member of the Communist Party of China and, of course, an atheist, Mr. Hsiu is not embarrassed to pose with a religious idol.

A warm and friendly man, Mr. Hsiu is expert on Soviet "hegemony." He interprets the latest developments in China's conflict with Hanoi; he is prepared to discuss the realpolitik of China's rapprochement with West Germany. Mr. Hsiu exemplifies the Chinese penchant to quantify: "Stalin did seven good things and three bad things." He speaks of "the three loyalties" and "the five and the seven categories of bad elements."

While many great archaeological treasures have remained buried, the renowned Fei Lai Feng Buddhist rock carvings were selected for preservation and restoration.

Religious observances are officially condemned; churches and temples have been converted into warehouses. But it is known that twenty Catholic bishops are still alive. Church officials in the free world were stunned to receive news in December 1978 that a handful of Chinese Catholics openly participated, without harassment, in Christmas Eve mass at the Church of the Immaculate Conception in Peking. Throwing puritanical ways to the winds, the International Club (possibly mistaking Christmas Eve for New Year's Eve) held a dance from 10:00 P.M. to 5:00 A.M.

## 39  *Forbidden Intimacy*

Here in the Forbidden City in the center of Peking is a pavilion where the imperial concubines were housed. Only eunuchs were allowed in the palace to protect the women and to educate the emperor's children. Ambitious families were known to have their sons castrated so that they might infiltrate the power structure within the palace or gain the emperor's ear by influencing a royal offspring.

A young couple sit in the pavilion enjoying a moment of privacy. Since Liberation, the Chinese have been dogmatic prudes. Until 1978, it was unusual to see a young man and woman publicly seated so close together. Any sort of premarital intimacy was discouraged. Now, China is deemphasizing her puritanical standards. However, most couples still do not marry until the woman is over 25 and the man is over 27, a firm convention which necessarily reduces the overall birth rate.

Recent poster campaigns have demanded a liberalization of the delayed marriage rule and a relaxation of sexual taboos. Officials insist there is no such thing in China as premarital sex ("young citizens are too busy nation building").

But always, there are contradictions. In a country with the moral standards of Victorian England, the pharmacies still sell male silkworm tonic for impotence.


## 40  Shanghai Fish Production Commune

While carp production is the chief undertaking, pigs, chicken, mink, ducks, and oysters are also raised. Everything here contributes to the needs of something else. The mink eat leftover fish heads and intestines. The fish eat pig droppings. Pigs eat chicken droppings. Peking ducks are force-fed and allowed to swim once a day, lest they work off their fat.


## 41  Hangchow Commune

Outside of Shanghai, the signs on the columns of this people's commune read:

"We follow Chairman Hua intensely.
"We uphold the new march of revolution.
"We grasp these big movements intensely."

The dreary rhetoric does injustice to the most staggering reform in the economic history of mankind: full employment, guaranteed medical care, and full rations of rice in the agricultural commune.

Gone are the landlords wearing elegant gowns, keeping their fingernails several inches long, and doing no labor whatever. Gone, too, are their wives spending long hours arranging their hair in elaborate chignons and dressing in silken finery.

Life is so much better, but there is so far to go. Chairman Hua has revealed that the individual grain ration in 1978 was no higher than in 1955. Peasants will be paid 20 percent more for their grain in 1979, one of the new governmental incentives to increase production.


## 42  Lotus Feet

This woman is unable to walk without help from her grandchildren or a solicitous stranger.

The practice of footbinding spanned 1,000 years. It was an excruciating process begun in early childhood. The bones of the instep were gradually bent until they met the heel. The crippled child had to hobble painfully on her big toe and her heel. These broken stumps were known as lily or lotus feet. They became a mark of beauty and were thought to be sexually exciting. Eventually, with progressive bandaging, the foot was reduced to a length of three or four inches.

Footbinding was officially outlawed in 1911, but, in some backwater areas of China, the practice continued until 1949.

A few women of poor peasant descent escaped the painful process altogether, as did the boat people of Canton and the powerful Manchus.


## 43  Three Generations

Three generations of a Chinese family enjoy a summer afternoon in a Hangchow park. Grandmother and father are both smokers, but political pressures and education will turn the son against smoking before he reaches adulthood.

Grandmother has stuffed the toes of her cloth slippers with cotton. Slipper production orders from Peking do not take account of the existence of bound feet.

Bound feet are fast disappearing as are the memories of past oppressions. Children and young adults of China born since the 1949 Revolution have never seen a rich landlord. They are constantly reminded: "The old society gave your mother nothing but a cangue* around her neck and fetters on her feet."

## 44  Peking Grandmother

A grandmother with bound feet comforts her grandson in a Peking park. The baby buggy, tumbrel-shaped, is a design unique to the Peking region.

Old people throughout China raise grandchildren and do light housekeeping. Partially to solve the unemployment problem, forced retirement is early by western standards. In Soochow, the elderly care for sick silkworms.

## 45  Grandfather and Baby

Peking has had three consecutive poor harvest years. This used to mean famine: babies crying, children abandoned, adults stampeding the trains carrying grain. Under extreme conditions—cannibalism.

The poor grain-growing conditions this past year on the north China plain hold no threat to this Shanghai granddaddy. China has 50 million tons of grain in storage—about five times the amount of its annual purchases from the United States, Canada, and Argentina.

## 46  Junk on the Whangpoo River

A Chinese junk sails toward the Yangtze River on the ebb tide. Chinese superstition produces the traditional junk with great eyes and head to resemble a sea monster. The mat sails have bamboo ribs and conjure up visions of gigantic seagoing bats. The design of the junk has not changed in centuries.

Any fool knows these man-made floating monsters will scare away sea serpents and other creatures of the deep.

## 47  Farmers in Peking

Chinese peasants visiting Peking pass through the Gate of Heavenly Peace. These tourists have the unmistakable long angular faces of the northern Chinese.

Chairman Mao is still a national religion. He is universally esteemed, beloved, and idolized. Yet to be laid at his door is responsibility for the purges and killing of millions of people for no greater crime than being "aristocratic," "elitist," or "landowner." The upheaval of his Cultural Revolution sent engineers to work in rice paddies, closed the universities, and jailed thousands of intellectuals.

As the Chinese nation now mourns and rehabilitates the martyrs who died in disgrace during the most recent purges of the late 1960s, a kind of national schizophrenia has set in. Hundreds of millions of Chinese people must struggle with the once inconceivable idea that "even Chairman Mao made mistakes."

Reaffirming the stature of Mao, a plenary session of the Communist Party of China declared on December 23, 1978:

> "The session emphatically points out that the great feats performed by Chairman Mao Tse-tung in protracted revolutionary struggle are indelible. . . . It would not be Marxist to demand that a revolutionary leader be free of all shortcomings and errors. It also would not conform to Comrade Mao Tse-tung's consistent evaluation of himself."

## 48  Peasant Carrying Sacks of Chaff

Many years of economic self-sufficiency separated China from two commodities she needed most: imported agricultural equipment and foreign chemical fertilizer technology. For a country which still produces 87,000 new babies every day, this was a near catastrophe. Only the compulsive work drive of the Chinese peasant labor brigades saved the day.

---

*A huge table-like wooden collar, so large that the victim could not feed herself.

This peasant carries sacks of chaff which may be used to heat a home or fire a kiln. Nothing goes to waste:

"Grow grain and vegetables, but if they won't grow, grow fruit trees. If trees won't grow, then grow berry bushes. If bushes won't grow, encourage the production of weeds, to feed the pigs and to add to the compost."

—La Wao Fu
Vice Director, Linhsien County Commune
Honan, China

### 49 Water Buffalo and Plow

Such agricultural technology as exists in China today is the two-wheeled, hand-driven, water-powered tractor. The peasants call it "the iron ox." Few things in China escape politicization. One brand of tractor is called "The East Is Red."

Only a very small part of China's agriculture is mechanized. In the rice paddies, the long-horned water buffalo pulling a crude wooden plow with an iron tip introduced 2,000 years ago remains the standard method of turning the soil.

The "new modernization" calls for the purchase of 4 million foreign-manufactured combines and tractors. But where and how is China to find the trained mechanics to maintain this equipment?

### 50 Aged Man with Palmetto Fan

"An aged man is but a paltry thing,
A tattered coat upon a stick, unless
Soul clap its hands and sing."

—William Butler Yeats
"Sailing to Byzantium"

### 51 Women in Harness

In every country, there are animals in harness. But China is a country where the human being is a beast of burden, a constant reminder that the People's Republic is still very poor and underdeveloped. Straining every muscle, the peasants and city workers pull loads of fodder, wood, and waste—often twenty or more times their own weight. Always, there is an efficient cadence in their steps.

Here, two young women appear to trot ahead of their load like circus ponies. This running gait makes the pulling easier.

Since the primacy of Vice Premier Teng Hsiao-ping has been established, China is being more candid about her backwardness. Declares Teng, who is 75 and "about to meet Karl Marx": "If you have an ugly face, it's no use pretending you are handsome."

### 52 Woman Soldier

Women serving alongside the men in the Army is not a recent phenomenon. Equality of the sexes in the military was practiced during the 1850s when the Taipings took and held Nanking and many other walled cities.

This woman is a proud member of the People's Liberation Army, where she not only defends her country but repairs its streets and harvests the crops.

### 53 Pataling Pass

Highways in China are primitive. Trucks are small, rarely over 5 tons. Canal and river transport is limited. Nearly 70 percent of China's freight goes by rail, almost entirely steam- and diesel-powered. Now, like railway men everywhere, China's officials want to convert to electricity.

The sign reads: "Stop! Look! Cross!" The train has stopped a half-mile from the Great Wall at Pataling Pass. The contours of the land have changed, and, suddenly, as the train climbs north from the plains of Peking, rocky hills appear like giant molehills. Suddenly, the traveler finds himself in the mountains. Across the hills is the great Gobi Desert.

48

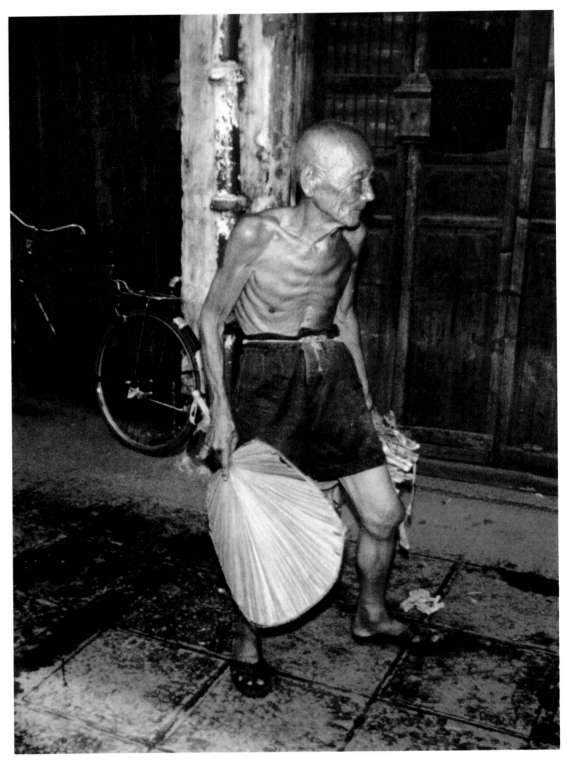

50

54

57

58

60

## 54  Sampan on Canton's Pearl River

The Pearl River is the traditional home of the red-sailed junks and gray-sailed sampans. Shown is a sampan typical of the "houseboats" on which tens of thousands of outcast Chinese boat people lived for centuries. Life offers a few amenities now. Notice the house plant on the port side.

Since the late summer of 1978, a new kind of boat appeared on the Pearl River. It is a diesel-powered 30-knot hovercraft ferryboat. This sleek white boat whisks sixty-three passengers three times daily on its 75-mile run south from Canton to Hong Kong.

## 55  Overcrowded Kwangtung Housing

The older housing in Canton, capital of Kwangtung Province, is architecturally elegant but severely rundown and overcrowded.

Since the Revolution, births have been held down by eclectic but firm public policies for birth control. This included free tubal ligation, state-supplied birth-control pills, and counseling on family planning in rural areas by the celebrated "barefoot doctors." Late marriages have been encouraged, and it is reported that harsh sanctions, such as loss of ration books, have been levied on families producing more than two children.

In December 1978, an official radio broadcast from Kwangchow reported a serious increase in the birthrate. One reason given was the bad example of certain party leaders who have produced six (and in one case seven) children. It is likely that increasing use of financial incentives to encourage greater production run counter to policies to hold down births. Families in China correctly conclude that greater family income will result from giving birth to more producers.

China has taken no census in more than two decades. Foreign demographers estimate the population has reached over one billion persons, nearly a quarter of all humanity. The U.S. Census Bureau puts Chinese births at 31 per 1,000 population and deaths at 11 per 1,000 every year. This would give China an annual growth rate of 2 percent, a rate at which the population would double in thirty-five years.

## 56  Winnowing

Peasants near Hangchow operate a traditional winnowing machine which separates the grain from the chaff. The stalks are beaten against straw mats which are supported by wooden sticks to form a box. Leftover stalks are used as fuel for firing brick kilns.

Chinese agriculture employs human waste as fertilizer. This "night soil" is emptied from communal toilets and transported in carts or trucks to a large concrete holding tank. There, it ferments anaerobically for three months. Harmful bacteria and spores are killed during the storage period. At the end of the fermentation process, the precious fertilizer is diluted with water and applied to the crops. The problem of intestinal parasites has been eliminated by the extremely high temperatures produced during the night-soil fermentation process.

## 57  Shanghai's Watermelon Market

China is famous for her succulent fruits. Red-fleshed peaches come in June, and juicy watermelons are harvested in August; they are followed by pears and, in the late fall, by rosy persimmons. In winter come oranges and tangerines, which are unforgettably sweet.

The price of fruit is regulated by the local communes and is uniform throughout a town. Informal rationing also occurs through long queues of citizens standing in line for hours, waiting for the fruits to be individually weighed. Here, the vendor cuts the watermelon; the buyer usually devours the bright red, or sometimes yellow, meat on the spot. He spits the seeds out and throws the rinds into a special trough. The rinds are hauled to the country to be fed to pigs.

## 58  Shanghai Waterways

Some 2,000 years ago, China was the world's leading maritime power. Her ships sailed the Orient, including the Islands of Japan. Latest anthropological theory is that the Japanese today are offspring of Chinese colonists who sailed to the archipelago about 200 B.C.

The name Shanghai means "To the Sea." The city is part of the world's largest metropolitan area and is the most central port along China's 11,000 miles of coastline. It has a capacity considerably greater than the Port of New York. Ships from all diplomatically recognized nations jam the berths. Eighty percent of the cargo handling is mechanized.

The city is dominated by water traffic. Soochow Creek bisects Shanghai and flows into the Whangpoo ("Yellow Beach") River. The Whangpoo in turn runs into the Yangtze. On Soochow Creek, the creations of Chinese nautical design are a tour de force. Series of makeshift barges, one tiny lead boat and eight mongrel companions fishtail behind like sections of an awkward centipede. The waterborne traffic jams are more tangled and less easily corrected than those on land. Barges of coal snake in and out of sampans, transporting small loads of fish, produce, families, coolie hats, oars, all a jumble. A nightmare for navigators and paradise for the sightseer. The colors of the buildings and water are Venetian: pinks, beiges, and lavender.

The People's Republic has the third largest navy in the world. According to recent counts, there were forty-eight submarines (possibly one nuclear powered but not missile carrying), at least five guided missile destroyers, and 220 torpedo boats. Chinese naval vessels may be seen along the Whangpoo and Yangtze. Photography in these areas is forbidden.

The resumption of full diplomatic relations between the United States and China reopens trade between the two nations but still does not permit United States flag vessels to enter China. Chinese vessels are still subject to attachment in the United States for claims of United States citizens against China for property expropriated in China after the Communist take-over in 1949. As long as the issue remains unsettled, China does not grant immunity to United States vessels entering China waters.

## 59 Neighborhood Spying

The armbands identify two older persons who watch "vigilantly" for erroneous behavior or deviant political beliefs.

Mutual spying is traditional. Today, almost everyone belongs to neighborhood committees. The committee holds weekly discussion and study groups. The themes are criticism and self-criticism.

"Letters of emotion" are written. Citizens pass around samples of these letters. Everybody makes ten copies. Sometimes, no one reads the letters; they just count them. For example, Wo Kuen hands in six letters of emotion. She is ruled to be acceptable. But Chen Chou, who hands in only two, will be scrutinized further.

Promotion to a better position has been the reward for turning in one's neighbor or accusing him of holding incorrect or unreconstructed beliefs.

The revolutionary committee controls every facet of human life. It issues the food-ration tickets, the movie tickets, and permissions to visit relatives and friends outside of the work area. A woman who wishes to have a child may be obliged to seek permission of the committee. Unless the committee grants permission, a third child may be denied a place in the nursery. When issuing ration tickets, the committee may even forget to count the unauthorized infant. Neighborhood sanctions are more effective than could be any birth-control order from Peking.

## 60 Street Scene Outside the Imperial Palace

The 100-acre Forbidden City is the great monument to China's past. From this extravagant labyrinth of buildings did twenty-four emperors express contempt or condescension for the European "big-nosed hairy ones" who were the "barbarians from the Western Ocean."

So withering was China's determination to get rid of "things old" that the towering arches and other monuments which used to grace the ancient city have been torn down to make way for wide avenues and dreary Stalinesque buildings.

Beneath the City of Peking, the people have built a complete underground city. There are roads, streets, first-aid clinics, and facilities for food preparation and food storage. Gigantic blast doors separate the different sections of the shelter system.

Deep water wells which maintain a constant temperature of 57° Fahrenheit, emergency power generators, and air-filtering equipment have been included in this system of civil defense which the government claims can accommodate most of the population of Peking.

"If the Russians come, we can fight them from our tunnels," one guide told the authors. "Dig tunnels deep, store grain everywhere, and never seek hegemony," said Chairman Mao. The sign outside the Palace reads: "Long live the Unity of the World's Friends."

## 61 Train Guard

Diesel locomotives are green, red, sleek, and as nostalgically appealing as Lionel toy trains. The passenger trains travel at 40 to 50 miles per hour over smooth roadbeds. So far, no bullet trains.

Railroad workers are reputed to be the most rebellious of the Chinese labor force; but to the foreign observer, they appear to be industrious and docile. Trains remain heavily guarded.

## 62 Ping Pong

These eight-year-olds have been playing ping pong since they were old enough to hold a paddle. No rational Westerner, however proficient, would challenge them to a game, for they will thrash him straight away and then inform him—with Chinese sense of good sportsmanship—that *he* won.

## 63 Woman With Umbrella

The "self-moving vehicle" is the work horse of Chinese transportation. In greatest numbers (2 million in Peking) is the black unisex bicycle. The price is $100 (U.S. currency) plus a certificate of need from a brigade head.

This woman travels in state in the more sophisticated tricycle cart. Her great black umbrella, which most citizens carry, is a work of folk art. Made of bamboo and oiled silk, the umbrella costs about $1.50.

The vast majority of urban Chinese travel in buses and trolleys. The fare is about 1 cent. It is obligatory for a Chinese citizen to stand and offer a seat to a foreigner.

## 64 The Peking Summer Palace

It was here that during much of the last century the Dowager Empress Tz-u-hsi was served ducks' tongues in lots of fifty stuffed melons, fried magnolia, and lotus flowers—and crushed pearls as a preventive medicine.

In 1850, the annual budget for running the court: about $12 million.

## 65 T'ien An Men Square

The quintessence of "People's Grandiose" architecture, T'ien An Men Square is an expanse of 98 acres, larger than Red Square in Moscow. Peking's great ceremonial square is the center stage of all Chinese political theater. Here occur the controlled public demonstrations informing the people that they will learn modernization rather than Maoist dogma or that henceforth they will be motivated by incentives rather than by ideology.

In T'ien An Men Square, the people of China will be told whether they are to have more freedom or less freedom. The Square is the center of manipulated street corner democracy where a citizen hears bombastic rhetoric about "the dogheads" who will be "smashed" because they have been caught on what, for the moment, is the wrong side of party orthodoxy. In this great square, western journalists first learned the amazing news of the normalization of relations with the United States.

All this happens in the world's worst climate. Peking is a city of icy winter winds, broiling summer heat, and choking dust storms in the spring.

62

63

68

70

73

74

Some 800 million Chinese people live in rural areas mainly in agricultural co-operatives. These units vary in size from 10,000 to 40,000 people. The dwellings range from caves to mud houses to adobe huts, to a few up-to-date dormitories.

The vital importance of the commune as central to the economic plan was reaffirmed in a statement issued by a plenary session of the Communist Party of China on December 23, 1978: "Rights of ownership by communes, production brigades, and production teams and their power of decision must be protected effectively by the laws of the state."

Peasants are urged to own their own pigs and to produce and sell a small supply of vegetables privately. The Party statement is specific on the subject of private enterprise. "Small plots of land for private use by commune members, their domestic side occupation and village fairs are necessary adjuncts of the socialist economy." When a man dies, his pigs and cattle are left to his family, one of the few visible examples of capitalistic practices.

Brigade and village are synonymous terms. People *live* and *work* together as members of a production team. They perform stoop labor as their ancestors did before them. The elderly remain fully integrated in family and village life. Those too old and frail for heavy field labor stay in the village and help with food preparation and the care of small children.

## 67 *The Shoemaker*

For old men, the most popular summer hangout is the sidewalk. There is bamboo furniture for every activity: a stool for Chinese chess or cards, a lounge chair for dozing, and a regular bamboo chair for gossiping.

This gentleman is a shoemaker. The sectional bamboo clothes-drying racks are traditional. The authorities find these racks backward and somewhat embarrassing. Peking ordered them stowed away when President Nixon first visited China. Foreign guests are not taken to these rundown neighborhods. The tourist buses travel by them at breakneck speed.

## 68 *Woman With Garbage Pails*

This Shanghai woman has an aristocratic air, most definitely not a peasant face. Daughter of a landlord or other privileged person, she is still undergoing reeducation. Traditionally, persons with "bad class" backgrounds have been "reconstructed" through menial work such as sweeping lavatories, and hauling "night soil." They may still receive unequal wages and may be denied free brigade medical services. Only a few years ago, young people whose grandparents belong to the wrong class were paraded through the streets wearing dunce caps. At least 50 million citizens are victims of "reverse discrimination" because of "rich peasant" and other upper-class backgrounds. Their children have been denied music lessons, and other educational opportunities. They cannot join the People's Liberation Army or become Communist Party members.

China has been gradually dismantling many of the punitive policies of the late Mao Tse-tung. Two years ago, urban young people were being forcibly resettled in the countryside. The slogan then was: "Setting up a People's commune is like going to heaven." Today, the youths from the city are more likely to be going to school.

## 69 *Hauling Logs*

The backwardness of modern China shows in her almost universal use of human beings as draft animals.

Most workers are permanently attached to a production team or brigade. Supervised by revolutionary committees, these units closely supervise work behavior and political attitudes. Reflecting the current relaxation in political dogma, these committees have lost importance; in most cases, they are being withdrawn from factories.

Excepted from official scrutiny are the Chinese carters who spend long unsupervised hours on the road. Ross Munro, the noted Peking correspondent, reports that the carters are among the most individualistic people in China: "They cuss and joke as the mood moves them, apparently unconcerned about what anybody thinks."

The bicycle lashed to the logs permit this Chekiang worker to ride back for another load.


## 70   Pedal-Operated Sewing Machines

Sewing is a profession that requires some manual dexterity but is not physically demanding. It is a task often assigned to semiretired persons.

A Chinese proverb says: "A needle is better than a bar of gold." In modern terms, this means Chinese officials have at last consented to permit the labels of American high-fashion firms to be sewn into clothes made in China.

China is the largest single source of cotton textiles imports into the United States. In 1978, shipments were running at the rate of 170 million yards a year. China now has the petroleum base for synthetic fibers and soon will be producing them in competition with Japan, Hong Kong, and Taiwan. Cotton goods are in short supply and are strictly rationed in China.

Worker protest has been known to occur. This crime is called "active hooliganism" or "anarchosyndicalist deviationism." In other words, a strike.


## 71   Mary Cross and the Gang of Forty-Four

Photography is hindered in Chinese cities by enormous crowds of curious children. The authors were more of an oddity than pandas in the zoo. Irresistibly, the children follow these strangely dressed visitors staring at their clothes, imitating their speech, and laughing hilariously. Many of the adults have never seen a western face or blond hair.

Most Chinese object to being photographed. They spot cameras right away, dart inside their houses, or hide their faces behind palmetto fans.

Notice at the far left the little rascal with this mock curtsy to the photographer. All one August afternoon in Canton, he hurled catcalls and kept calling "Mary." There is a kind of game between photographer and Chinese citizen. If your camera catches him before he ducks, there are no hard feelings.

Officially forbidden to photographers are anti-aircraft guns standing in fields outside of Shanghai, military vessels, armament plants, and aerial photographs. There is no rule against photographing primitive means of agriculture or backward living conditions, but most Chinese transport hurtles the photographer and tourist alike at breakneck speed through areas where agriculture is done by stoop labor or where city dwellings belie the claims to progress and modernization. If one catches a good shot here, it is luck and fast film.


## 72   The Gate of Heavenly Peace

Peking loudspeakers are rapturous about the "Four Modernizations": "Red flags fly everywhere. . . . The masses of the people are high-spirited. . . . Everywhere in our motherland orioles sing and swallows dart. . . . Hot tears rush to our eyes. . . . We are in the process," the loudspeakers now scream, "of comprehensively grasping and applying the Four Modernizations."

China's current "four modernizations" program (modernization of agriculture, industry, scientific research, and the military) represents a victory, for the moment, of the policies of the late Chou En-lai.

In 1975, Premier Chou, in his last public appearance, outlined plans to improve China's agriculture by 1980. This, he said, would "turn a poverty-stricken and backward country into a socialist one with the beginnings of the prosperity in only twenty years or more." The current Vice Premier Teng Hsiao-ping, Chou's protegé and disciple, is believed to have been the author of the plan. Only 4 feet 11 inches tall, Teng, whose name means "Little Peace," is a tough pragmatist, intent on adopting the technology of western capitalism. To appease the radical Maoists who would faithfully adhere to "pure" socialism uncontaminated from the taint of outside aid, Teng declared: "In the process of achieving the Four Modernizations, we must be good at comprehensively and accurate grasping and applying the thought of Mao Tse-tung." The Four Modernizations are radically un-Maoist. Only through the once-forbidden buyers credits arranged with international banks can China acquire tractors and large combines from capitalistic countries such as Germany and the United States. Modernization of industry will require internationally syndicated loans in the hundreds of billions. Scientific research, banished from China during the recent Cultural Revolution, will call for computer technology and assistance borrowed from the advanced Western capitalists. The modernization of China's hopelessly outdated military may not proceed without hardware from Stuttgart and Seattle. The high Chinese army officials, who have made military hardware shopping trips to European countries, salivate in anticipation; of course, they support Teng's policies. This, for the moment, gives Teng the upper hand over Chairman Hua Kuo-feng, Mao's titular successor.

As always, China finds scripture to justify what she wishes to do. The authority is Lenin, as interpreted by the still esteemed Joseph Stalin:

"In 1921 Lenin . . . recognized that the best among all the feasible measures which could be taken was to attract foreign capital, to use it for the development of industry. Unquestionably that was the correct way."

## 73  The Portable Food Cart

Even more than Americans, the Chinese eat on the run. If the citizen is too busy to go to a hot-food canteen, the portable food cart comes to him. This one belongs to a communal brigade which makes silk cloth. Inside the cart are breadlike steamed dumplings called "man tu," a starchy staple in northern China.

For centuries, China has had a reputation for exquisite cuisine. Nothing is wasted in Chinese cooking, from the lining of a pig's stomach to sea slugs and hen's feet. Everything is saved and prepared in a creative way. Recent announcements in the *People's Daily* suggest that prepackaged, quick, convenience food is on the way. Instant rice and dehydrated fruit will speed both the consumption and preparation of food but will destroy the traditional standards of culinary excellence.

Salads and uncooked greens are never served. Vegetables are fertilized with the "night soil" of human waste.

## 74  Swordplay

It is 5:00 in the morning. Every available bit of open space is occupied by citizens doing t'ai-chi-ch'üan, the ballet, swordplay, and trance exercise which has relaxed Chinese nerves for centuries.

The bookstore sign announces the newest thaw in the Cultural Revolution: "Let 100 flowers bloom; let 100 birds sing."

Don't bother to go in the bookstore in the background. There is still nothing there but Maoist tracts and revolutionary posters. Peking has announced the end of a ten-year ban on seventy international writers, among them Aristotle, Plato, Shakespeare, Balzac, Swift, and Mark Twain. But their works are difficult to find. The fact is that the bookshops have never recovered from the ransacking they took at the hands of the Red Guards during the Cultural Revolution (1966-1970).

A livelier variety of literature, including American fiction, may be found at Peking University, where student favorites are *Catch 22* and *Huckleberry Finn*.

## 75  Father and Son

Among young children and parents, the overt display of affection is common. When the child reaches preadolescence, hugging and kissing stops. Even at home, a mother or father will rarely embrace a teen-aged son or daughter. Closeness and love remain, but not conspicuous touching.

In Chinese tradition, sons are still expected to support elderly parents. The parents who give birth to female children are encouraged to keep trying until they have a son, a guarantee of welfare in their old age. Standing at his right is this young father's equivalent of social security.

## 76  Commanded to Return on Time

A visit to the Great Wall is the favorite outing for members of the People's Liberation Army. The baggy, ill-fitting uniforms have undergone "Chinese ironing" (sleeping on one's clothes to press them). The officers wear a loose jacket with four pockets. The privates have only two pockets. There is no other external insignia. It is difficult to imagine this crew deploying sophisticated photo-intelligence systems, ballistic missiles, and countercity nuclear weapons.

An officer issues an admonition to a platoon of PLA troops to be back to the truck on time after an excursion to the Great Wall.

## 77  Solitary Soldier

A solitary member of the People's Liberation Army sits atop the battlements of the Great Wall. This fortification has protected China (more or less) from her enemies for 2,200 years. In some locations, it served only as a convenient highway for troop transportation.

## 78  Children's Nursery at the Chin Sheng Silk Brocade Factory

Mothers work and Chinese children are cared for at kindergartens. The state nursery is a constant reminder to the parents that, in Mao's words, "Your children are not your own. . . . They are the future of China."

The loving and dedicated "aunties" who care for the toddlers at the Tu Chin Sheng Silk Brocade Factory teach the children to use their potties in unison.

## 79  Shanghai Social Hour

These Shanghai boulevardiers are thoroughly enjoying a midafternoon tea break. In China, people usually share, but each man has his own teapot. Each seems oblivious to the cinema posters which advertise political films such as tales of a high-living commune leader whose daughter committed suicide when her father got involved with "capitalist roaders" and other bad elements.

## 80  Bamboo Water Pipe

At one time, a huge number of men in China were opium addicts. In the last century, European interests used the drug as a weapon for pacification and political control. This man does not have an opium pipe but rather holds an antiquated bamboo water pipe, a favorite of the rich landlords prior to liberation. The pipe also serves him as a walking stick.

## 81  Storybook Grandmother

Supporting herself on a bamboo cane, this fairy tale grandmother hobbles through a Hangchow park on tiny bound feet. Wearing an old-style shirt buttoned on the side, she carries two buns and a palmetto fan.

The Chinese sense of mutual support runs deep. Someone will help her into the bus. Younger Chinese often try to shield the elderly from being photographed. Respect for old people is a powerful force in contemporary China. There is no stigma attached to being old. In cities, old people's homes have been constructed for those who have no children to care for them. They have been named "Homes of Respect for the Aged."

## 82  Popsicles

For a few pennies, popsicles are for sale in every Chinese city. The flavors are lemon, orange, and black bean paste. The street vendor has no formal refrigeration; each batch of popsicles is wrapped in a cotton quilt.

76

78

80

84

86

88

## 83  Washing Rice

The Peking Government has recently embarked on a propaganda campaign to convince the northern Chinese that it is in their best interest to give up noodles and switch to bread, a more nutritious staple. But in the south, rice continues to be the mainstay of the diet.

The 1978 grain harvest was poor. China is importing increasing amounts of wheat, corn, and soybean oil from the American and Canadian farm markets.

If the grain allotment for each of China's one billion people were increased by a pound per person per week, China's needs would increase by 20 million tons a year. This is a sum equal to the entire annual wheat consumption of the United States. Clearly, if Chinese diets are upgraded, it will not be easy to readjust to any more years of disappointing harvests.

## 84  Cyclists at the Ming Tombs

Near each large city that receives foreign guests, the Chinese have restored one or two monuments.

Thirty miles north of Peking is the Sacred Way or Avenue of the Animals, originally used for funeral processions of Ming rulers. The statues date from the fifteenth century. The body of the dead emperor moved down a 4-mile route to the gate of the chief tomb. Of the thirteen Ming imperial tombs, only one has been opened and restored. As most tombs and important sites have been precisely identified, Peking could, if her priorities so required, mobilize the necessary labor and rapidly produce the world's most exciting archeological discoveries.

These cyclists ride past a kneeling and a standing lion and a kneeling and standing "xie chi." The latter is a mythological feline with a mane and horn reputed to produce good luck.

The Ming Dynsty lasted from 1368-1644. Of the sixteen emperors, thirteen lie buried in this area.

## 85  Baskets on the Way to Market

Puffing hard on their cigarettes, these Chinese workers protect a load of recently woven baskets on a three-wheeled flatbed tractor truck.

## 86  Old Woman in Courtyard

The government has built new housing, but the majority of Chinese citizens prefer to live in an old-style house with a courtyard rather than in the newly built standardized dwellings.

Here in her Peking courtyard sits an old Chinese woman dressed in traditional black silk overblouse and trousers. Her feet are not bound, which suggests that she was born of a peasant family which needed its female children as workers and could not afford the luxury of foot binding.

Located on a "hu-t'ung" (small side street), this old house, designed to open onto a central courtyard, used to house a single family. Now, it has been converted into a multiple-family dwelling, with several families sharing the same kitchen and bath.

The spittoon is a common sight in private homes and public buildings. The Chinese plead climate when questioned about their crude spitting habits, which usually ignore the cuspidor.

Western television teams have acquiesced in Chinese Government requests to cut scenes of Vice Premier Teng displaying his considerable skills in the Chinese art of spitting.

## 87  Worker With Rubbers

The aged worker wears the traditional shiny Cantonese cloth jacket. It keeps him cool in the summer. His children probably insisted that he not leave the house without his rubbers.

Feeling strong affection and gratitude for the labors of their parents, they recall the following wisdom of the late Prime Minister Chou En-lai: "When you are drinking the water, don't forget the people who dug the well."

### 88 Woman Pulling Garbage Vats

The worker's cart is only one example of an infinite variety of ingenious Chinese vehicles—all based on the principle of the wheelbarrow. Mankind's greatest tool was invented by the Chinese ten centuries before it appeared in the West. Garbage will be taken to feed pigs. Two-wheeled carts of this type are not allowed to appear in Peking. They are bad for the national image. Throughout other regions of China, they are commonplace.

### 89 Pumpkins

The hair standing straight up suggests a vitamin deficiency, perhaps refuting the government's claim to a universally balanced diet.

Pumpkins, harvested in July, are a staple item for the Chinese family.

### 90 Tai Ching-chuan

Tai Ching-chuan, our interpreter and companion, employed by China International Travel Service, is suave, dapper, warm, well-groomed, and highly intelligent. We told him that in our country we thought he could be a ladies' man. He said: "Excuse me, I think it is time for some tea." When we asked about China's relations with Vietnam, he said the same thing. Mr. Tai was consistently tactful but unswervingly dedicated to the proletarian revolution. Even before normalization of relations, he was a true ambassador of goodwill toward the United States.

### 91 Cadre Mother

The woman shown here with her daughter belongs to the "cadre class" of very serious people. These are officials, persons in charge of communes, bureaucrats, propagandists, and the like. The "cadres" have certain privileges, such as possessing the coveted national ration coupons allowing them to buy rice in another city. But there are disadvantages also. The cadres arrive in a new position carrying a kind of "book of life" which details family history for three generations (no landlords allowed) and fitness reports prepared by other officials. As for new jobs, they go where they are assigned. According to Peking observer Ross Munro: "They are not interviewed; they are observed."

This woman is probably a party member. Party members are zealots who are over 18 years of age, observe the discipline of the party, and execute its decisions. To join, one must be proposed by two members and then be examined for political correctness. One must intensively study Marxism and Leninism.

### 92 Hunkered Down

The peasant on the right sells green apples to tourists at the Great Wall. Each apple is sold by weight as determined by the old-fashioned scale next to his basket of fruit. The white band painted on the tree behind the young soldier is not a marker to keep cars from running off the road. There are no cars. It's a whitewash mixed with insecticide to protect the tree from pests.

### 93 Peasant Smoking

One-third of adult Chinese smoke cigarettes, one of the few pleasures left to relieve the tensions and monotonies of routinized Chinese life. The government produces —sometimes for export—some twenty brands of cigarettes. Sales of cigarettes in China are taxed at 60 percent, a mystery to foreign economists since the government not only sets the price but collects all the revenue from cigarette sales.

As part of the current campaign to stamp out smoking, the origins of the vice were laid at the doorstep of the now-banished Gang of Four. Pinning the blame on leaders who have fallen from grace will be difficult. Even the revered Chou En-lai, the patron of Vice Premier Teng, was a heavy cigarette smoker. Teng has also been caught smoking by western photographers.

One stanza of a current catchy children's antismoking jingle illustrates the politicization of every facet of Chinese endeavor:

"Esophageal cancer must be thoroughly conquered.
"The pernicious influence of the Gang of Four must be wiped out.
"Putting prevention first is very important.
"We prevent and treat cancer for the revolution."

### 94 Members of the Largest Army in the World

Here are the ordinary rank and file of the People's Liberation Army. Before liberation, soldiers in China were corrupt—often not much better than roving brigands. Quartered with and living off the people, they took daughters of peasants for sexual gratification. Military officers were "high livers," extorting what they could from the wealthy landlords. Today, army officers again have become an elitist aristocracy. They ride in expensive cars and travel first class on trains.

### 95 Ch'ing Dynasty Vase and the Arts in China

A polychrome famille rose vase from the Ch'ing dynasty, Chien-Lung period (1736-1795) stands in the summer palace outside Peking. Seen through the iron fretwork is a People's Liberation Army soldier. He has come to the Summer Palace as a tourist. In China, soldiers wear their uniforms even when not on duty.

Hungry for culture and variety in their humdrum lives, the Chinese flock to museums and restored tombs and palaces to stare rhapsodically at the artifacts and treasures that make up their rich cultural past. Priceless art objects are frequently displayed without guards.

Since the Cultural Revolution, Chinese opera and other arts have concentrated on themes that would further the cause of Chinese socialism. The Peking Opera Company is again able to produce traditional operatic performances based on the fantasy-filled Chinese fairy stories from olden times. Provincial opera companies have also been permitted to substitute boy-meets-girl themes for didactic socialistic themes. These revisions have been slow in coming, and it is hoped that the recent changes in Peking's policies will become lasting and will spread to the film industry. There have been no movies presenting art for art's sake and diversion merely to please the citizens. Propaganda films have been likely to recount tales of industrial workers increasing production or of wicked landlords greedily hoarding rice for their storehouses.

At last, a few foreign films are being shown in Peking. They are starting with Charlie Chaplin's "Modern Times" and "The Hunchback of Notre Dame." A Japanese X-rated movie about prostitution was shown, a truly earthshaking event in a puritanical country.

Acrobatics are a popular but infrequent pleasure for a populace which jams the Peking Circus when it is in town. The emphasis seems to be balancing stacks of acrobats on the backs of bicycles. Political themes have been as intertwined with acrobatics as with other performing arts.

### 96 Chinese Pragmatism

American child-development specialists who have studied Chinese nurseries mostly agree that Chinese children faithfully meet the expectations of their parents and "aunties" and grow up to be calm and dutiful schoolchildren.

The boy on the right is partially toilet-trained. The hatch opening in the crotch of his pants is a marvel of Chinese pragmatism. He can do the job unassisted!

### 97 Multiple Mothering

"For the ego, for the personality to develop, the infant needs to experience satisfaction and challenge at his own pace. But nowhere has it been demonstrated that for survival or mental health, the satisfactions, challenges, and frustrations must all originate in the same person."

—Bruno Bettelheim
*The Children of the Dream*

Skirts and dresses, the former symbol of bourgeois decadence, have recently reappeared.

## 98 *The Four-Pronged Hoe*

In the old days when food was scarce and in lean years of poor harvests, the common salutation was not "How are you today?" but "Have you eaten?"

Two agricultural workers walk to the shade on a two-hour lunch break. Except for the noon break, there is no escape from the dawn to dusk regimen of drudgery. Almost never are they out of range of the loudspeakers in the fields which stridently exhort them to toil "with vigor" for all the people of China.

The four-pronged hoe carried by the worker on the right is a fair statement of the backwardness of Chinese farming. Agriculture dates to about 3000 B.C. in the valley of the Hwang Ho River. But the country has progressed little beyond the ox, the water buffalo, and the hand-held plow.

## 99 *Barefoot Doctors Make Housecalls*

Before 1949, tens of millions of people died in the rice paddies from scourges of typhoid, smallpox, and cholera which could have been prevented by rudimentary public health programs. Faced with the staggering problem of providing medical care for 700 million rural Chinese, the Peking Government decided to concentrate resources on the training of tens of thousands of paramedics. These are the celebrated "barefoot doctors." Paramedical training lasts up to two years and includes the use of Chinese herbal medicine, basic anatomy, courses in physiology, simple surgery, acupuncture, and general diagnostic technique.

There is no elitism among the Chinese paramedics. Barefoot doctors prepare their own medicines and are expected to do ordinary farm and factory labor. About 25 percent of their cases are complex and are referred to more highly trained physicians.

The prodigious efforts of China's public health system have been largely successful. Unlike other third-world nations, where large portions of the population are afflicted with parasitic diseases, most of the Chinese appear robust, rosy-cheeked, and vigorous. Medicine is not entirely socialized. In many cases, doctors are not free. Major surgery could cost as much as two weeks' wages.

## 100 *Memories of the Old Regime*

The memories of China's old people are a rich repository of links with the past. Only these venerable grandparents can recount with credibility the stories of oppressive conditions under the rule of mandarins and landlords. The old people alive today witnessed starvation, slavery, infanticide, and footbinding. It is they who verify legends, make the past real, and provide content and purpose for the dreams of a new China.

## 101 *The Shanghai Waterfront*

Looking toward the Shanghai waterfront from the Whangpoo River, the building on the left with the pyramid-shaped roof is the Peace Hotel. Once chic and fashionable, the playground of the smart international set, it is now faded and tawdry. In the uninviting lobby stand rows of chunky, overstuffed electric blue armchairs, each draped with three protective lace antimacassars. The chairs look like fat, tired dragons, no longer able to belch fire.

92

94

98

100

102

The most exciting feature of the hotel is in the bar. If the bartender takes a fancy to you, he pushes a button on the side of a big wooden box. Two panels then slowly part like a curtain in Radio City: lo and behold, a magnificent 10-inch black-and-white TV set. The program is Chinese opera: "The Monkey King Defeats the White Goddess"—considerably less tedious than "Sailing the Seas Depends on the Helmsman." Finally, China is starting to enliven and vary the choice of TV programs.

The building on the right of the picture is the State Bank of China, a slightly revisionist, if not renegade, institution which is developing (according to the precepts of Adam Smith, rather than Karl Marx) large tracts of valuable property in Hong Kong.

Like the Federal Reserve Board in the United States, the State Bank of China functions as China's central banker. It also operates 30,000 commercial branch offices throughout China. Under various names, the State Bank of China controls two dozen commercial banks in Hong Kong, London, and Singapore. The central control of banking, like monopoly control of the means of production, is a necessary element of state socialism. Seizing the banks of St. Petersburg was as critical to Lenin's revolution as taking control of its power stations.


## 102  Hot Lunches

The communal sinks provide a central meeting place for working women in the rural communes. Toilets and other plumbing are normally shared by several families.

Every working day, the women carry aluminum lunch boxes to work. At midday, they heat up their lunch pails containing rice and vegetables. Hot meals are considered essential. After work, they wash out the lunch boxes in the concrete sinks.

Individual dwellings in the communes are primitive, usually constructed of concrete with outdoor piping. Each unit has simple cooking facilities, a small living room for the adults, and tiny side rooms for children and grandparents. Standard equipment includes a wooden table, a bamboo chair, a calendar, and possibly a few family snapshots which hang on the wall. The once obligatory portrait of Mao is now optional.

The government allots each family two bars of soap and two light bulbs a year.


## 103  Chinese Footwear

In their choice of footwear, these northern Chinese peasants reflect poverty as well as individuality. Workers choose between sandals, tennis shoes, soft cloth slippers, canvas shoes and rubbers. High military or government officials have leather shoes.


## 104  The Badminton Game

At 6:00 A.M. on the streets of Peking, a slightly unorthodox game of badminton. The age of the participants does not dampen their enthusiasm. If one is mobile, exercise is required.


## 105  The Fan and the Tea Table

In summer, the streets are the parlors of the people. Drinking tea is a ritualistic pastime. It brings socializing and a feeling of well-being.

> "The most outstanding characteristic of Eastern civilization is to know contentment, whereas that of Western civilization is not to know contentment."
>
> —Hu Shih
> *La Jeunesse Nouvelle*
> April 1918

## 106 Cannons From the Opium Wars

North of Peking, Chinese tourists examine antique cannons which were used against the British during the Opium Wars.

So secure was China in the early nineteenth century that the celestially ordained emperor dismissed the British Ambassador from Peking in 1816 without even granting him an audience. By 1842, the gunboats of Britain, upholding principles of "free trade" (primarily for the sale to the Chinese of opium production from Bengal) had forced open the Chinese ports. By the end of the century, the whole China coastline was in European hands.

## 107 Wung Vegetables

The peasants who live and work in the vegetable production communes are often among the most prosperous groups in the country. The communal farmers take their crops to city markets and sell them at a price fixed by the government.

Shown here are so-called Wung vegetables. These are prepared with smashed garlic and preserved bean curd. It is a normal sight throughout Chinese cities to see big piles of string beans and other vegetables lying on a sidewalk.

The woman's prosperity shows in her possession of a wristwatch, a treasured possession in China. She has set up shop in a small free market in a narrow Cantonese street. She will supplement her cash income with extra money earned by selling produce from her private plot.

## 108 The Cloisonné Vase

A thousand or more skilled craftsmen work in this arts and crafts factory in Peking. Their wages have always been higher than compensation paid factory workers with lesser skills. In fact, pure Marxist wage equality has never prevailed. Now, the official edicts of the party, implemented in early 1979, officially call for "payment according to the amount and quality of the work alone."

Individual creativity in the arts is discouraged in favor of efficient production from a standard mold. Producing almost entirely for export, they work on highly stylized cloisonné, jade carvings, painted snuff bottles, and lacquered bric-a-brac.

There is no danger of theft of the large chunks of uncut jade which are casually stacked in the factory yard.

On the wall inside the main entrance to the factory, a large character poster announces the latest score, which in this country is the number of workers in the factory who own sewing machines and bicycles.

108